This Candlewick book belongs to:

_____

_____

_____

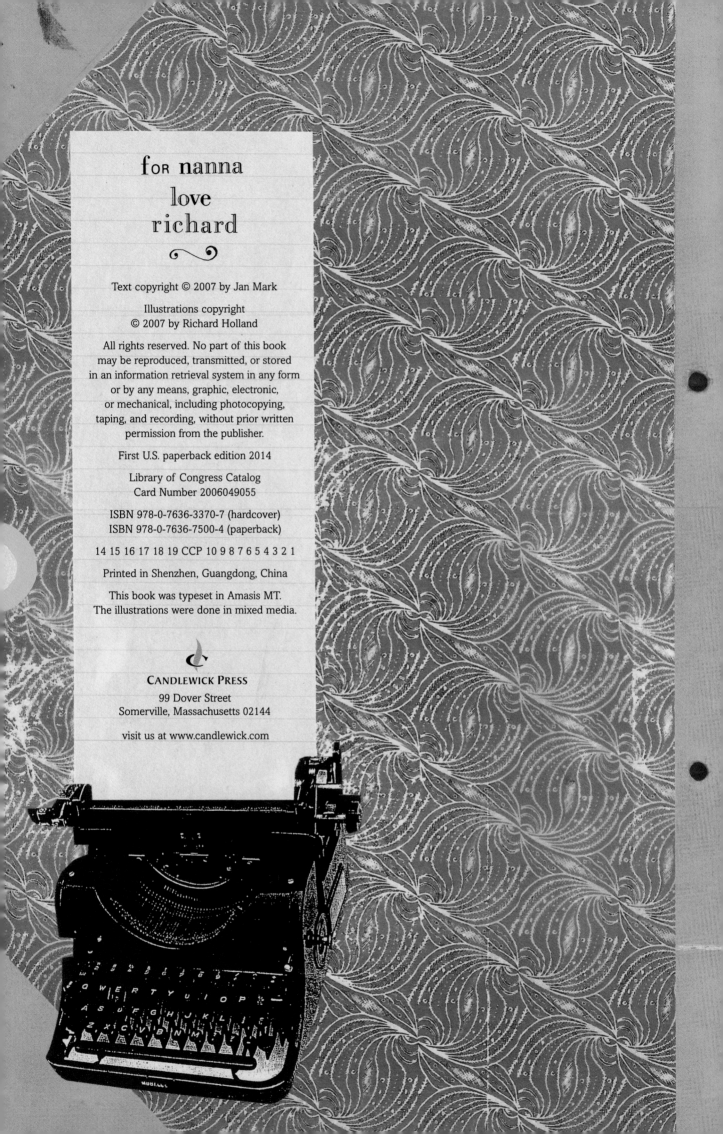

for nanna
love
richard

First U.S. paperback edition 2014

Library of Congress Catalog
Card Number 2006049055

ISBN 978-0-7636-3370-7 (hardcover)
ISBN 978-0-7636-7500-4 (paperback)

14 15 16 17 18 19 CCP 10 9 8 7 6 5 4 3 2 1

Printed in Shenzhen, Guangdong, China

This book was typeset in Amasis MT.
The illustrations were done in mixed media.

CANDLEWICK PRESS
99 Dover Street
Somerville, Massachusetts 02144

visit us at www.candlewick.com

The Museum Book

A Guide to *Strange* and *Wonderful* Collections

written by

Jan Mark

illustrated by

Richard Holland

Chapter One

Suppose you went into a museum and you didn't know what it was. Imagine: it's raining, there's a large building nearby with an open door, and you don't have to pay to go in. It looks like an ancient Greek temple. Temples are places of worship, so you'd better go in quietly.

But inside it doesn't seem much like any temple or mosque or church you have ever been in. That is, it looks a bit like all of them, but the furniture is out of place. Perhaps it's a hotel; it has fifty rooms, but there is only one bed, although it is a very splendid bed. Apparently Queen Elizabeth I slept in it. Or perhaps there are fifty beds, but they are all in one room and you can't sleep in any of them. There are red velvet ropes to keep you out.

Farther down the corridor you notice a steam locomotive. It's a train station! But there is no track except for a few yards that the engine is resting on, and already you

have seen something else. Across the hall is a totem pole that goes right up to the roof, standing next to a Viking ship. Beyond it is a room full of glass cases displaying rocks, more kinds of rocks than you ever knew existed, from diamonds to meteorites. From where you are standing, you can see into the next room, where the glass cases are full of stuffed fish; and the next, which is lined with shelves of Roman pottery; and the next, which is crowded with birds; and after that, lions and giraffes and pandas and whales.

It must be a zoo.

But when you go and look, you find that all the animals are stuffed and their eyes are glass. At least they still have their skins on, unlike the creatures around the corner, which are nothing but bones held together with wire. You know what *that* one is: a *Tyrannosaurus rex*. You've seen him on television. And then you notice some people standing around wearing clothes from a hundred, two hundred years ago, a thousand years, two thousand—right back to people who are not wearing any clothes at all, just bits of fur.

You'd like to ask someone what is going on here, but they aren't real people at all: they're made of wax.

At least *they* haven't been stuffed.

You start to find your way back to the place where you came in, past the dinosaurs, past the fish and the rocks, but there is so much to see. Here is an airplane, a whole, real airplane, hanging from the ceiling. There is a room with weapons on the walls and suits of armor standing around . . . and a World War I tank. On that table is the very first telephone in the world, and over there is a sheep with two heads. What's in that cabinet?—No, you don't really want to look at those. Someone has been collecting teeth. His name was Peter the Great, Tsar of Russia, and he pulled them out himself. He was an amateur dentist. Not many dentists do it for fun.

For a moment you feel nervous. Is Peter the Great still around, looking for more teeth to add to his collection? Would he want yours? He is probably not the type to ask politely. But, you tell yourself, there is no need to be nervous. These look like very old teeth. Peter the Great must have lived hundreds of years ago. (You're right; he died in 1725.) But now you can't help noticing that *everything* in this place is old, or dead, or old *and* dead.

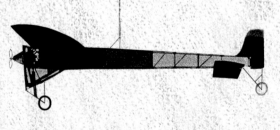

ring ring

Just then you see someone walking toward you who isn't dead—you hope. He is wearing a uniform with a badge on it that reads *Guide.*

"Enjoying yourself?" he says.

You say, "Where did you get all this stuff?"

"All?" he says. "These are just the things we show to the public. Down in the basement there's a hundred thousand times more. Do you know," he murmurs, "we've got *twenty-seven* two-headed sheep?"

"But why?" you ask. "Why do you have *any* two-headed sheep?"

"Because people give them to us," he says. "And so that you can look at them. Where else would you see one? Where else would you be able to see the mummy case of King Tutankhamun, the first plane to fly the Atlantic, the first train engine, the last dodo, a *diplodocus*, the astrolabe of Ahmad of Isfahan (an example of the oldest scientific instrument in the world), chicken-skin gloves, the lantern carried by Guy Fawkes when he went to blow up the British Parliament buildings, a murderer's trigger finger—?"

"But where am I?" you say. "What *is* this place?"

And he says, "It's a museum."

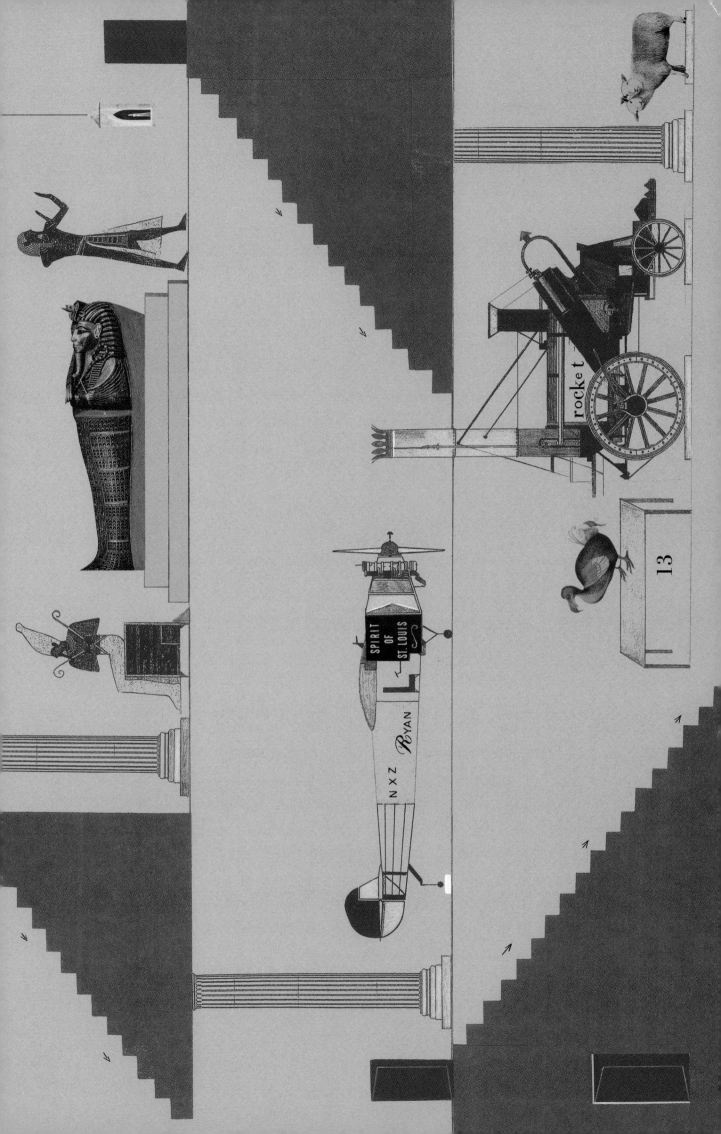

Chapter Two

550 BCE sounds like a long while ago, and it is, but even as long ago as that, someone built a place to keep old and interesting things in. Her name was Princess Bel-Shati Nannar and her building was in the lost city of Ur (in what is now Iraq), but it is unlikely that she called it a museum.

Words are not just useful noises. They grow out of other words and attach themselves to things that have no names. A museum was a place where the Muses lived.

Who?

To find out who the Muses were, we have to go back, beyond the gods of ancient Greece and the temples they were worshiped in, to the beginning of time. (No, not the Big Bang; that's science.) This is a myth, one of those stories people used to tell when they tried to answer difficult questions like:

Where did we come from?

What is a rainbow?

Where does the sun go at night?

Why does the moon get bigger and smaller and sometimes
    disappear altogether?

What is the moon, anyway?

Before the gods, there were the Titans, children of Gaea and Uranus, the earth and the sky. There were twelve of them, six sons, and six daughters. One of the sons was named Chronos, and he was time itself. One of the daughters was named Mnemosyne, and she was memory.

Mnemosyne married Zeus, chief of the gods and the son of Chronos, so she was actually his aunt, but gods and Titans did not have to worry about things like that. They were together for nine nights, and Mnemosyne had nine daughters.

They were called Clio, Euterpe, Thalia, Melpomene, Terpsichore, Erato, Polyhymnia, Urania, and Calliope, which was too much for even the gods to remember, so they were known as the Muses.

Polyhymnia

Calliope

Melpomene

Thalia

Urania

Erato

Terpsichore

Euterpe

Clio

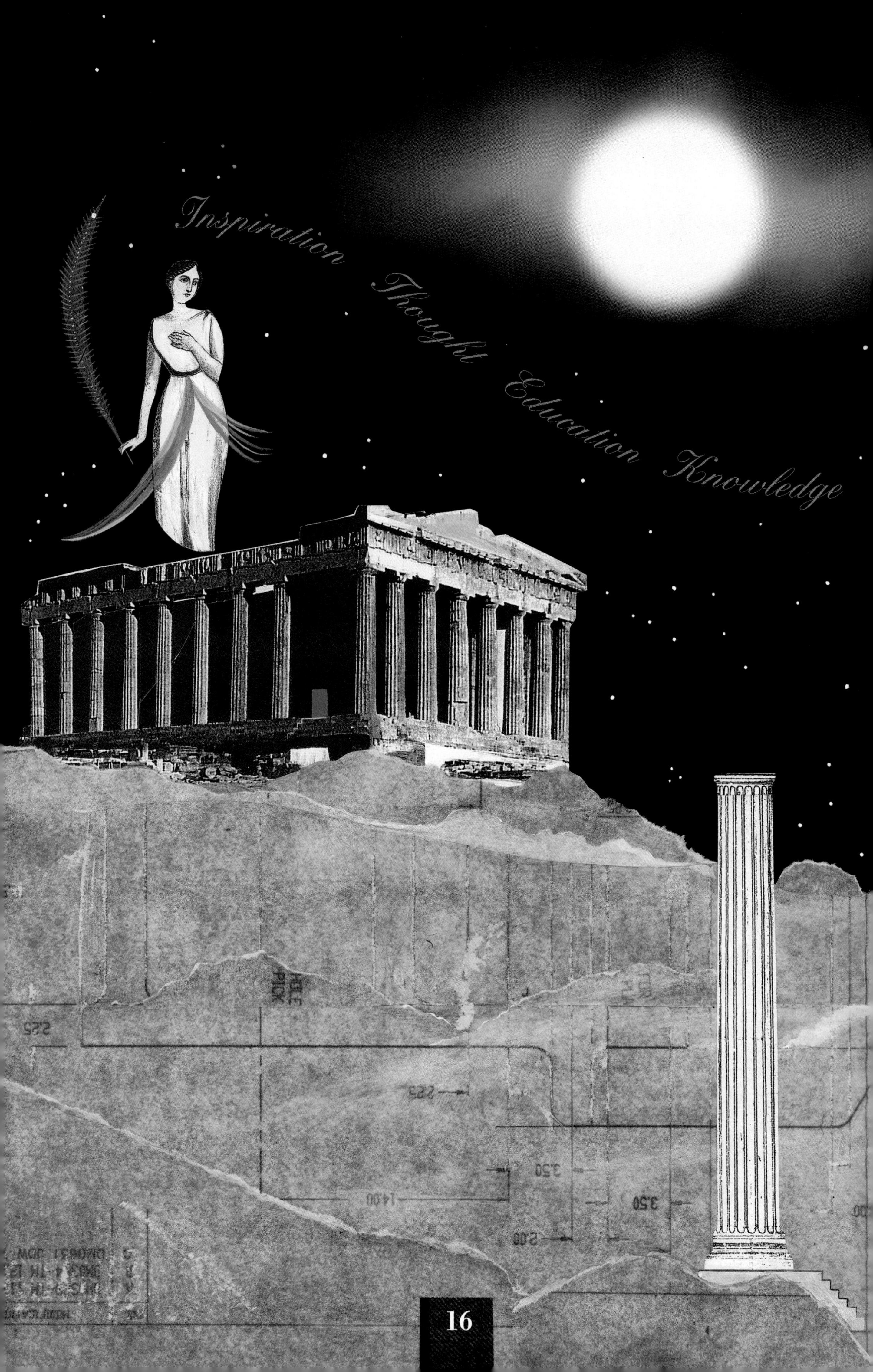
Inspiration Thought Education Knowledge

The word *muse* is still around now. If you listen to music, you are hearing the art of the Muses. Between them, they took care of all the arts: history, music, comedy, tragedy, dance, poetry, astronomy, and eloquence—what we would now call the gift of gab.

They lived among the springs and meadows of beautiful Mount Helicon, and when the gods were feasting on Mount Olympus, the Muses went along as a choir to entertain them, but at night they would come down to earth and humans would hear their voices. Their dull, human minds would be filled with new and exciting thoughts, and the next morning they would go off and tell stories or write plays, poetry, and songs. When friends asked them where they got their ideas from—people always ask writers that—they would answer, "From the Muse."

The first museum was called The Museum because it was the only one. It did not have old, dead things in it. It was the university building of the city of Alexandria in Egypt, a palace where people could learn and study, and the men who built it thought that it would make a perfect home for the Muses.

It was a very long while before the second museum was built, and it happened almost by accident. No one ever sat down to invent the kind of place you visited in chapter 1, but once it existed, people decided that *museum* was exactly the right word for it.

Chapter Three

Back in the Middle Ages—say 1000 to 1500 CE—Christians collected holy relics. They either carried the relics around with them for good luck (although they did not call it that) or put them in the local church. If it was really lucky, a church might have a whole saint, but most of them had to make do with bits of saints: a finger bone or a kneecap or a toenail. The next best thing to that was something the saint had actually used or touched.

A lot of these things were fakes. Between 1387 and 1400, Geoffrey Chaucer wrote *The Canterbury Tales,* about a group of people going on a pilgrimage to the shrine of the saint Thomas à Becket. One of them was a crook who sold pigs' bones as holy relics and claimed that he had part of the sail of Saint Peter's fishing boat. People like this sold little bottles of

white liquid they said was the Virgin Mary's milk or passed off splinters of wood as fragments of the True Cross, the one that Jesus was crucified on. And even in those days, people like Chaucer were beginning to suspect that if you collected all the bits of wood that people were claiming came from the True Cross, you would end up with enough wood to build Noah's Ark.

The Abbey of Saint-Denis, near Paris, had so many holy relics— probably real ones—that it needed a special place where people could look at them. This would have set visitors thinking: they might not have any relics of their own, but they might have picked up some interesting things on their travels, such as a long, straight horn that must have come from a unicorn, a couple of dragons' teeth, a strange, curled-up stone that might be a serpent's tongue, or a jewel from the head of a toad. Why not display them in a special place where other people could admire them?

In the end, none of these things turned out to be what people thought they were, but they were rare and interesting, and if they were rare and interesting, they might have special powers. Men who were particularly interested in special powers were alchemists and apothecaries. Alchemists were searching for the elixir of life, which would make people live forever, and for the philosopher's stone, which would turn base metals—like iron or lead—into gold. They never did find them, because such things cannot exist—although people are still trying to live forever—but they often made important scientific discoveries while they were looking. The great scientist Sir Isaac Newton was an alchemist.

Apothecaries were the people who came before pharmacists. Their shops were stacked with rare and interesting objects. Every self-respecting apothecary had to have a stuffed crocodile hanging from the ceiling. His shelves would be lined with dried plants, creatures pickled in bottles, corals, seashells, tortoise shells, and unusual stones. There was always a chance that oil of mandrake would help to set broken bones or that toadstones would cure the plague. There might even be a use for the crocodile. It looked so impressive; it must make extra-strong medicine. A stuffed crocodile was a must-have for an alchemist, too.

It is easy to laugh, but without these people leading the way, we would not now have pharmacies selling cheap cures like aspirin for ailments that once made life a misery.

Not all collectors were apothecaries and alchemists with shops and laboratories. Most kept their rare and interesting objects at home in beautifully decorated boxes and cupboards called "cabinets of curiosities."

Sometimes they collected too much for one closet; they would need a whole room. The Germans came up with a word for this:

Wunderkammer
Chamber of Wonders

21

Chapter Four

In the sixteenth century, an early collector named Ulysse Aldrovandi said, "Nothing is sweeter than to know all things." People who collect, no matter what the objects—teeth, starfish, fruit labels, trading cards— want to get them *all*, a full set. Men like Aldrovandi tried to get the whole world into a box. If they could only collect everything together, in one place, they might understand the secrets of the universe. These days we understand that the more we know, the more there is to find out. We will never "know all things."

By Aldrovandi's time, every collector wanted the most curious cabinet of curiosities, the most wonderful chamber of wonders, the biggest collection. A century later, things were really getting out of hand. The collections grew too large for boxes, too large for rooms. It was all very well for kings and rich men, as they had plenty of space, but not all collectors were kings and rich men.

Perhaps one day the collector's wife looked at her house, overflowing with fossils and dried toads and corals and plants and books and dragons' teeth, the stuffed crocodile and the nasty shriveled thing under the stairs that gave her the creeps, and said, "Either all that goes or I do!" The collector would think about this for a while and then find someone to take the collection off his hands.

either ALL ThAt goes Or I do!

he bigger the collection, the bigger the problem. In 1677, Elias Ashmole wanted somewhere to put his collection of old and interesting things. He had not collected them himself; they had been left to him by a friend named John Tradescant. John and his father were naturalists, and they traveled the world in search of new plants. They picked up a lot of other things while they were at it, and when Elias Ashmole inherited the collection, he had to find a place to keep it. He gave it to the University of Oxford—on the condition that they put up a special building to house it properly, and in 1683 they did. It is still there, in Oxford—the oldest existing museum in the world.

The Ashmolean Museum, as it is called, has now moved to a bigger site, and the original building has become a science museum. If you really do want to see the lantern that Guy Fawkes was carrying when he went to blow up the British Parliament buildings, this is where you will find it.

Robert Cotton, who lived a little while before Ashmole, and Edward Harley, who lived a little while after him, did their own collecting on a gigantic scale. Cotton put together a library of rare manuscripts. Harley married an heiress and spent his wife's fortune building up a collection of manuscripts, pictures, and curiosities. These enormous collections were difficult to look after properly. Much of Cotton's library was destroyed by fire, and Harley had to sell a lot of his possessions when he ran out of money. Both men were dead before anyone found a safe place to keep their collections.

Here comes Peter the Great again. At almost seven feet tall, he was hard to miss. He was also brilliant, energetic, ruthless, and mad. He thought nothing of the thousands who lost their lives building his city of St. Petersburg over a swamp, yet he himself died after wading into the icy sea to rescue people from drowning.

Peter was a collector. Some things, like the teeth and his stuffed crocodile, he collected himself. He also bought collections from other people and sent out agents to find marvelous things for him. He ordered his librarian to visit museums all over Europe to find out what was missing from his. He was interested in everything and, like Ulysse Aldrovandi, he wanted to *know* everything. When he planned a great fleet of new ships for his navy, he set out to learn how to build them for himself.

He thought that it was not enough to display thousands of rare and precious things—they ought to be chosen so that people could learn from them. So Peter opened his collection to the public. They did not have to pay at the door—he lured them in with glasses of free vodka—and today you can still see what they saw, along with many other things collected since, in the Kunstkammer museum in St. Petersburg.

Peter wanted people to be amazed by his museum, and they probably were, although they may not have learned much from it. It had a great natural history collection: stuffed elephants, stuffed people (and live ones), and a two-headed sheep. But you cannot find out much about things like this just by looking at them. After all, you can stand all day and stare at a two-headed sheep, but you still won't discover why it has two heads.

Chapter Five

One of the most important English collectors was Sir Hans Sloane, who offered his wonders and curiosities to the British government. The government, thinking of Elias Ashmole's special building, set up a lottery to raise money to buy the Sloane Collection, as well as Edward Harley's collection of manuscripts and the remains of Robert Cotton's library and antiquities, and to build somewhere to keep them. In 1759 they put them all in one building and called it the British Museum.

It is not the building that you can visit in London now, which went up in the nineteenth century and looks like a Greek temple from the front. The new Ashmolean looks like a Greek temple too, and so do a lot of European museums. At the time it seemed to be the right way to design a museum, a true home for the Muses.

There are more than 2,500 museums in the United Kingdom and at least 15,000 in the United States. Some of them you might not think of as museums at all. Kew Gardens, in London, and the Botanical Gardens in Sydney, Australia,

Lakenhal

Tower of London

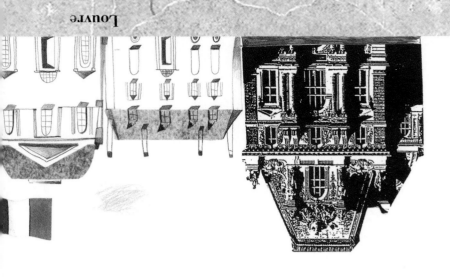

are museums of plants. A zoo is a living museum of animals. (The word *zoo* is short for zoological garden, and zoology is the study of animals.)

Some buildings are so remarkable that they *become* museums in themselves, such as Leighton House in London, the home of the Victorian artist Lord Leighton, who had it decorated in the style of Islamic art. The Lakenhal (Cloth Hall) in Ypres, Belgium, was destroyed in World War I, but it has been rebuilt just as it was and is now a war museum. The Chrysler Building in New York is a masterpiece of Art Deco style. The jail in Goderich, Ontario, is a museum because of its strange design, called a panopticon. The Tower of London is a museum, and so is the Topkapi Sarayi in Istanbul, Turkey, which was once a palace. The Louvre, in Paris, was also a royal palace. After the French Revolution, the new government opened it as a free museum so people could see that the treasures that once belonged to the king now belonged to the nation.

Topkapi Sarayi   **Kew Gardens**   **Chrysler Building**

Awhole town or city can be a museum. Athens and Rome are national capitals, but many of the great buildings from thousands of years ago are still standing, among modern highways and apartment buildings. Venice, in northern Italy, is a city where ordinary people live and work, but millions come from all over the world to see it because it is so old and beautiful. Venice is built on a lagoon; it has canals instead of streets. The buses are boats, called *vaporetti,* and even the firefighters travel by speedboat.

Unfortunately, the city may not be there for much longer. The seas are rising and Venice is sinking.

It would be hard to save Venice by taking it apart and rebuilding it somewhere else, but many outdoor museums are put together this way: by dismantling buildings from different places and putting them together in one place, so that visitors can see what life used to be like at a certain time in a certain place. The first museum of this kind was built at Skansen in Sweden in 1891. Now all such museums are known as Skansens.

Williamsburg, Virginia, has been frozen in time. In the early 1900s, modern buildings were torn down, old ones were restored, and those that had been demolished in the past were rebuilt so that the city now looks as it did in the eighteenth century at the time of the Revolutionary War. Places like this—and there are not that many of them—employ people dressed in costume, living and working as they would have at a certain period in history, who will explain what life was like at that time.

Places in the western world that once had heavy industry such as mining and steel production often become museums when the pits and factories close. The Coalbrookdale Museum of Iron, in Shropshire, England, is an industrial museum, and so is the Rüsselsheim Museum, in Frankfurt, Germany.

In many countries, the word *museum* is also used for an art gallery. The Guggenheim and Getty museums, in the United States, are art galleries, as is the Groeninge Museum, in Bruges, Belgium. And in Angers, France, there is an art gallery that is even more like a museum. When the sculptor David D'Angers died, he left all his sketches, notes, models, and tools to his hometown. From these, you can learn all about the man and his work while you look at his art.

Every time you open a dictionary, you are entering a museum of WORDS. You may sometimes see a word described as "obsolete." This means that it is no longer used; it is dead; you will find it only in old books or in the dictionary-museum. *Obsolescent* means that something is *going* out of use. Quick! Use it at once before it becomes extinct, like the dodo. You might be in time to save it. There is nothing worse for adults than going into a museum and seeing things on display that they remember using themselves—cameras, windup toys, telephones, the bus they used to catch to school. It makes them feel obsolescent, too. Words go out of use much faster than things. Think of the words that have died in your lifetime.

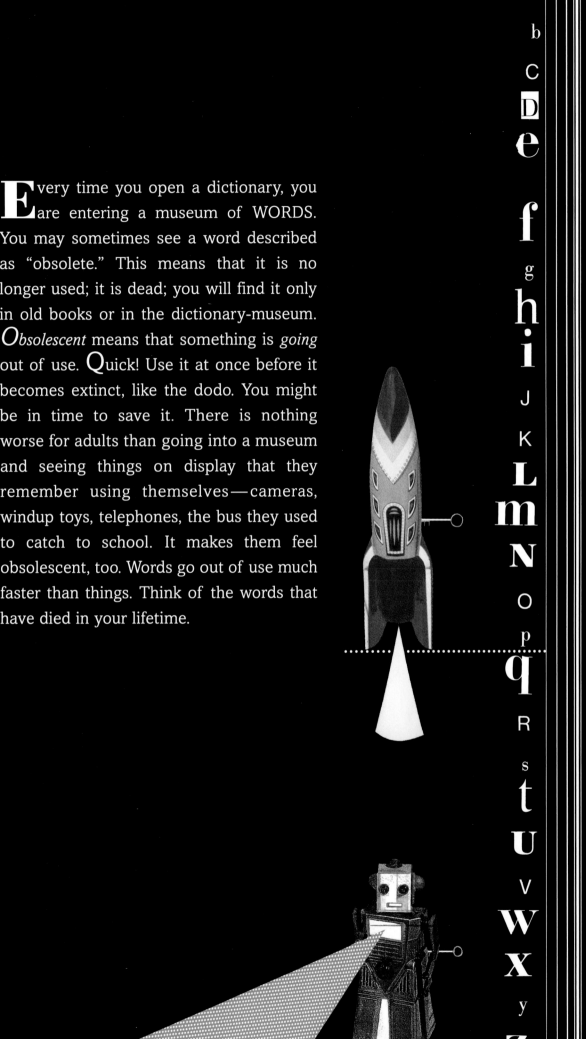

a
b
c
D
e
f
g
h
i
J
K
L
m
N
o
p
q
R
s
t
U
v
w
X
y
z

33

Chapter Six

Peter the Great's granddaughter, Catherine the Great, was also a collector. She was mainly interested in art and bought hundreds of paintings. She built the State Hermitage in St. Petersburg to hold them. It now owns three million items.

The empress Catherine was not so enthusiastic about Peter's curiosities. She knew very well that you cannot cram the world into a box or a room or even a palace. Ideas had changed since Peter's time. People were beginning to realize that while the *Wunderkammer* might be fun, in a way, nobody could learn very much from it.

Scientists saw that, in order to learn anything from these enormous collections, they would have to start sorting things out to see how one set of plants or animals or fossils was related to another. This is called classification.

A Swede, Carl von Linné, known as Linnaeus, came up with a way of classifying plants and animals. Almost a century later, the Danish professor L. S. Vedel-Simonsen thought of the idea of the "Three Ages of Prehistory"—Stone, Bronze, and Iron. Archaeology could start to be sorted out, too.

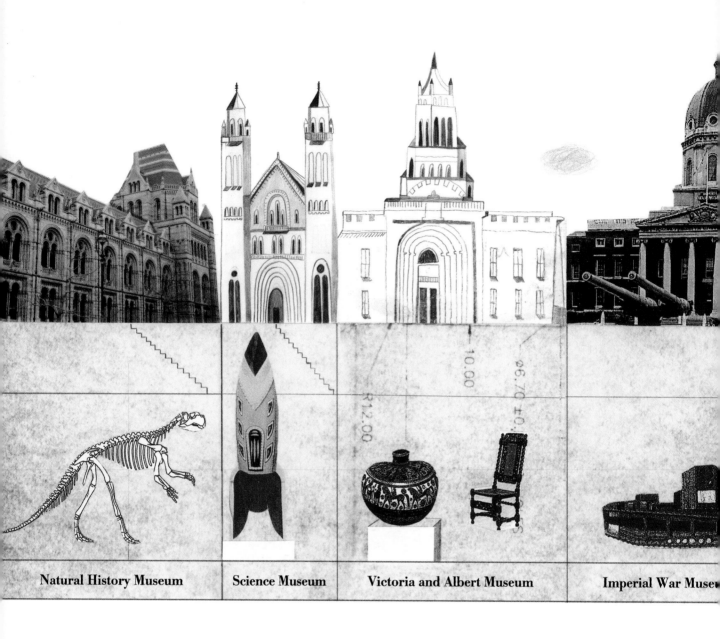

Natural History Museum   **Science Museum**   **Victoria and Albert Museum**   **Imperial War Museu**

By the end of the nineteenth century, it was understood that you could not fit the whole world even into a museum. In London, the British Museum moved its natural history exhibits into a new, specialized building, the Natural History Museum in South Kensington (which looks like a Gothic cathedral rather than a Greek temple), where you would go now if you wanted to see dinosaurs and rocks and stuffed animals. Behind it is the Science Museum, and if you were looking for the history of art and design—costume, furniture, pottery—you would cross the road to the Victoria and Albert Museum.

A "synoptic" gallery in a museum is a room showing different kinds of the same thing—fish or firearms or mummies or saucepans. But some synoptic collections need a museum all to themselves. If you were interested in military history and you were in Paris, you would go to Les Invalides. In London it would be the Imperial War Museum, and in the United States, it might be Gettysburg.

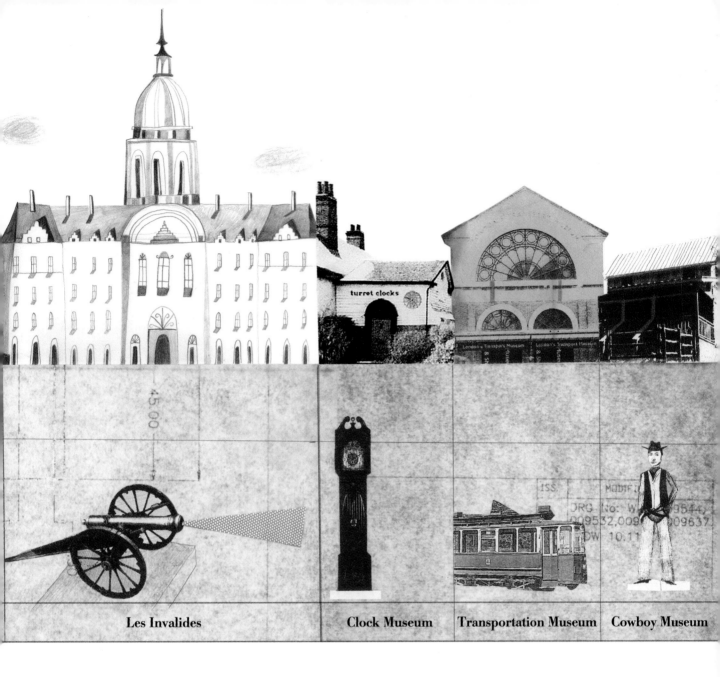

Les Invalides   Clock Museum   Transportation Museum   Cowboy Museum

There are synoptic museums all over the world: clock museums, transportation museums, agricultural museums, wax museums (try the Musée de Cire in Québec City, Canada, which is seriously creepy), ceramic museums, cowboy museums, computer museums, and medical museums. There are twenty-one specialty museums in London alone, including a dental museum, for people like Peter the Great, who are interested in teeth.

Are there no museums like the one you wandered into in chapter 1, that still have a bit of everything?

Yes, there are. In fact, most museums are like that, and there is sure to be one near you. It may not be full of strange objects from faraway places; it may be the local museum that tells the story of the place where you live. If so, if there is a two-headed sheep in it, then you can be sure that it is a local two-headed sheep.

If you own a rare and wonderful object, there are three things you can do with it. You can hide it away and gloat over it like a miser when no one is watching, you can show it to your friends as a special favor, or you can let everyone take a look.

Some people did hide their treasures—as they do today when they buy fabulously expensive paintings and lock them in bank vaults. But once there were museums—whole buildings filled with wonders—it seemed only sensible to let the public in to see them.

It was not easy to get into the first British Museum. After you'd booked in advance and hung about in the rain and then been rushed around the exhibits by a guide who could not tell you what they were, it could hardly have seemed worth the effort. The idea that a museum would be a place that millions of people might want to visit took a long time to catch on. Collectors could not believe that ordinary people might be interested in their collections, because they thought that ordinary people would never understand what they were looking at. Only very clever persons, they thought, would learn anything from seeing such very extraordinary objects. The idea that *anyone* could learn from going to a museum was quite a long while coming, too.

The first person to think seriously about this was a man named Lieutenant-General Augustus Henry Lane Fox, the Fifth Baron Pitt Rivers. Despite his impressive name, he started out as an ordinary army officer, testing a new rifle for the British Army. To understand the weapon better,

TWO
MINUTE
TOUR

he began collecting firearms. When his collection grew too large he, like Elias Ashmole, persuaded Oxford University to take it, and you can still see it in the museum that bears his name, along with an enormous number of things collected by other people such as Captain Cook, the explorer. The Pitt Rivers Museum, in fact, is rather like a huge *Wunderkammer* with thousands of curiosities, including a glass case with shrunken heads, which everyone wants to see.

Pitt Rivers thought that the British Museum was all very well for learned scholars to do research in. What he wanted was a museum where people could educate themselves about the past, just by looking around it. So he built one of his own.

Pitt Rivers was the first real archaeologist, excavating sites to look for clues to the past instead of tearing in with a pick and shovel in search of treasure and missing the really important finds because they looked like junk. He excavated in southern England on his own estate and built his museum there because he wanted to "make sense of history where it happened."

Chapter Seven

Not many big museums make sense of history where it happened. They are usually full of things that have come from somewhere else, very often things that have been looted in war or just taken away.

In the early 1800s, Lord Elgin took away some of the marble carvings from the Parthenon, an ancient Greek temple that stands on a hill above Athens. The Elgin Marbles are kept in that imitation Greek temple, the British Museum, and Greece would like to have them back. The British argue that if the museum had not been taking care of them, they would have fallen to pieces by now. This may be true, but the Greeks want to see these magnificent carvings where they were meant to be, in Greece.

LONDON 1448KM

It was not only carvings that were taken. Another thing that people are fascinated by is human remains. Many museums exhibit Egyptian mummies, the preserved bodies of people who died thousands of years ago. None of their descendants is around to complain, but there are also shrunken heads from South America like the ones in the Pitt Rivers Museum, and skulls of Australian Aboriginals and New Zealand Maoris—and some people do now want their ancestors sent home (though no one has claimed the shrunken heads). They do not like seeing them on display to the public—they think it is insulting.

And many of the mummies and other bodies were buried by people who believed that they would lie undisturbed for eternity, never to be seen again. They went to great lengths to hide their graves under tumuli, pyramids, and kurgans. They would be horrified to find us lining up to stare at them in glass cases.

Some exhibits in museums are models, or replicas, and if they are, it will say so, but some things that have been displayed were not even real in the first place. They were fakes, like the holy relics that Chaucer wrote about.

A famous Etruscan (pre-Roman) statue of a married couple was on display for years before someone discovered that it had been made in the nineteenth century. Many cabinets of curiosities contained mermaids. You can still see them. They look really fake to us now, but in the days when people believed in mermaids, they must have seemed like the real thing—except that mermaids are supposed to be beautiful. Sailors made them by joining the top half of a monkey to the tail of a fish, because they knew they could sell them to landlubbers who would believe anything.

One of the most famous fakes was the skull of Piltdown Man. For years it was thought to be the fossil of the "missing link" between humans and apes, what we now call the common ancestor. It was certainly that in one sense. It had been put together from a human cranium and the jaw of an orangutan. Even now, no one is quite sure who did it, but it fooled many scientists for decades.

famous fakes

Chapter Eight

Remember what the guide said in that museum where you sheltered from that rain—for every object on display there may be hundreds of others in storage?

What are they for? Why do museums keep all these things?

What else could they do with them? Throw them out?

The person in charge of a museum is the director. People who look after collections are curators. The word *curator* means someone who takes care. They do not want to throw anything away. They never know when they might need it.

There was once a clearing-out at the Ashmolean Museum, and some fragments of a dodo were taken away, because no one could see any point in keeping them. At the last moment they were rescued from a bonfire, which was just as well. The dodo, a big, flightless bird, was already extinct. Now you can see a reconstruction at the Natural History Museum in Oxford.

Species become extinct all the time, faster and faster, more and more. There must have been specimens in the old cabinets of curiosities that no one will ever see again. It is now illegal in many countries to collect birds' eggs, but once this was a popular hobby. So was collecting butterflies—and not many people would even *want* to do that now. But museums have collections of thousands of birds' eggs and butterflies left over from the old days, and we can still learn from them.

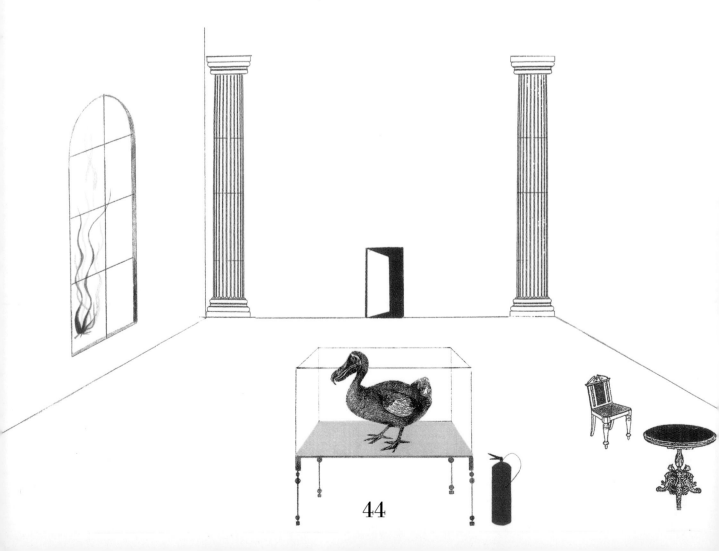

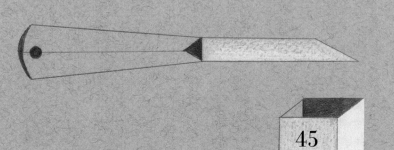

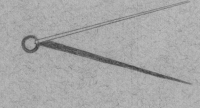

45

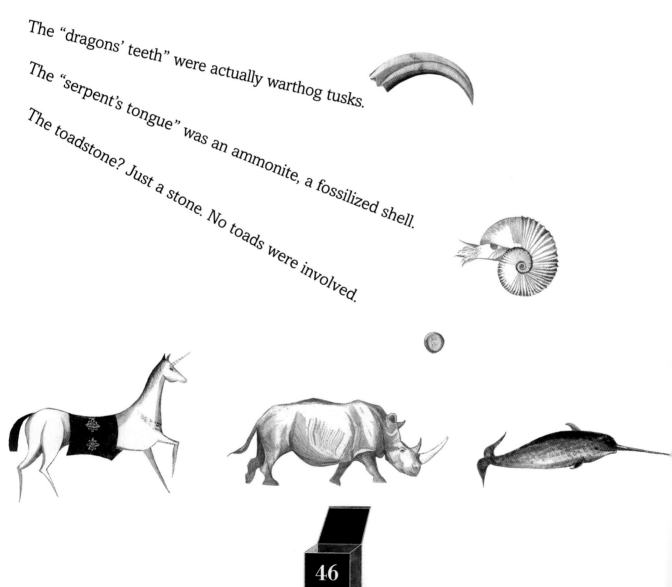

The cabinets and *Wunderkammern* were filled with things that people did not understand at the time and could not identify; they could only guess at what they might be. Saved in museums, these strange things were still there when people had the knowledge to work out what they really were.

Take the unicorn's horn, for instance. People had heard of an animal with only one horn, but they had never seen it. It was probably a rhinoceros, but as they had never seen one, they did not know that a rhinoceros's horn is on its nose. They thought it must grow out of its skull, as horns usually do, which is where the idea of the beautiful fantasy creature originated. Most horns grow in pairs, so people thought the long, single, elegant, ivory spirals must have belonged to unicorns. They turned out to be the tusks of narwhals, a kind of marine mammal like a dolphin.

The "dragons' teeth" were actually warthog tusks.

The "serpent's tongue" was an ammonite, a fossilized shell.

The toadstone? Just a stone. No toads were involved.

46

The unicorn's horn was an honest mistake and quite a reasonable one, if you think about it. It made perfect sense at the time. When archaeologists first began trying to reconstruct dinosaurs from fossil bones, they came up with some very odd-looking creatures, but not much odder than the real thing. We are still changing our minds about what the real ones looked like. When you see a TV show about dinosaurs, they are often shown in bright, glossy colors. This is guesswork. No one has any idea what color dinosaur skins were. All we find are bones turned to stone: fossils.

So it was not only people with cabinets of curiosities who got things wrong—we are all learning all the time. Collectors, curators, and directors all share the same belief: everything is interesting. Even if we do not know what something is now, we'd better keep it. Eventually someone will come along and discover what it is, perhaps not in our lifetime, but one day.

Once, when stones fell from the sky, people believed that the god Zeus was hurling thunderbolts. They did not connect them with the lights that burned across the sky at night, which they called shooting stars. Now we know that those are meteors, chunks of space debris burning up as they enter the atmosphere. The ones that fall to earth are meteorites.

The tiny arrowheads that turned up in fields were called elf bolts, obviously made by the fairies. In fact they were made by humans in the Stone Age—but how could people know that if they had never known that there was a Stone Age?

Museums are always running out of space. A lot of them are running out of money, too, and yet the collections keep growing.

You may know something about this yourself. If you are a collector, finding somewhere to keep your collection can be a problem. Stamps, postcards, and fruit labels are easy, since they can go in albums, but if your collection is made up of objects that are any larger it soon starts to take up space. It gathers dust. Your family might not like the kind of thing you collect. You may grow tired of it yourself, but so much effort and money has gone into it that you can't bear to get rid of it. If you collect books, you really have a problem. If you collect cars, you have an even bigger problem, unless you own a car museum, like Lord Montagu of Beaulieu.

But there is another kind of collection that everyone has, including you. It is in your head. Everything you have ever seen, heard, smelled, tasted, or touched is in there. Most of it has been pushed to the back, like the things in storage in a real museum, but an enormous amount is still there when you need it. You can get it out and have an exhibition whenever you want; you can spend as long as you like wandering around it. As you get older, many things that you did not understand when you first stowed them away suddenly start to make sense. Bring them back up from the basement. *Now* you know what they are.

Remember Mnemosyne the Titan, mother of the Muses? She was memory. Memory is your museum, your cabinet of curiosities, your *Wunderkammer*. It will never be full; there is always room for something new and strange and marvelous. It will never need dusting.

It will last as long as you do. You can't let the public in to walk around it, but you can take out the exhibits and share them, share what you know.

You will never be able to stop collecting.

48

Mom Dad cat
sat mat ball no
good bad
teeth house
shoes swing
apple moon sun
stars walk run snow
flower boat dinner book picture
song story friend garden park street
shops school nits television music airplane
radio blood bone heart thought painting
motor electricity theater map arithmetic god
lie death truth skeleton dinosaur gorilla dictionary
phantom recorder orchestra language opera algebra physics geology
history logic biology chemistry trigonometry archaeology paleontology astronomy
nanotechnology bigotry monochrome tragacanth amaranth terebinth labyrinth synthesis
synapsis pharmacopoeia dodecahedron chiaroscuro obsidian fulgurite disestablishmentarianism
quark phantasmagoria ai ohm cynocephalus jot ochlocracy floccinaucinihilipilification...

Glossary

Antiquities p. 28
Most people mean the time before the Middle Ages when they talk about *antiquity*. Antiquities are very old artifacts.

Archaeology pp. 35, 39, 47
The study of the past and, especially, objects that humans have made in the past. These are called artifacts. Paleontology is the study of fossils; these are not artifacts—unless they are fakes.

Astrolabe p. 12
An instrument for measuring the altitude of the stars (their height above sea level, rather than their distance from earth).

CE p. 18
The Common Era. History is usually dated BC (Before Christ), and AD (Anno Domini, the Latin for *In the Year of Our Lord*), because the people who invented the system were Christians. The Common Era is the dating system that everyone uses whatever their religion. BCE means Before the Common Era.

Ceramics p. 37
Pottery: that is, anything made of clay and hardened by baking it at very high temperatures.

Etruscan p. 43
The Etruscans were people from Etruria, an empire in central Italy founded almost 3,000 years ago. The first Roman kings may have been Etruscan, but eventually Etruria was absorbed into the Roman Empire.

Exhibition p. 48
A public display of objects or paintings that have been specially brought together—but anything being exhibited is on display, wherever it is.

Manuscript pp. 25, 27
Writing done by hand rather than printed. *Manus* is the Latin word for hand, *scriptus* for written. A manuscript can be one page or a whole book. Before printing was invented, all books were in manuscript form.

Mummy pp. 12, 36, 42
A dead body that has been preserved by drying. Many societies all over the world have made mummies—the most methodical were the ancient Egyptians—but mummification can also occur naturally in the right conditions.

Panopticon p. 29
A prison with cells built around a watchtower in the center so that prisoners would always be in sight of the warders. The word means all-seeing.

Prehistory p. 35
The time before written history. Only archaeology can reveal what was happening then. The geological past, when the earth's crust was still forming, is too long ago to be called prehistoric.

Reconstruction p. 44

Rebuilding, putting something back together, sometimes without knowing quite what it looked like in the first place. The dodo was reconstructed from a skeleton using a painting for guidance.

Shrine p. 18

A place where holy relics are kept so that people can visit and be near them.

Species p. 44

A group of plants or animals that are very similar to each other. Lions and jaguars are cats, but they are from different species. Modern humans are all one species, *Homo sapiens*. *Homo erectus* and *Homo sapiens neanderthalensis* (Neanderthal man) were early human species that died out.

Tumulus p. 42

A mound of earth raised over a burial site in prehistoric times. A kurgan is similar to a tumulus but very much larger. Kurgans are found across Russia. During the Battle of Stalingrad in World War II, the Mamayev Kurgan was known as Hill 102 because it is 102 meters high.

Two-Headed Sheep pp. 10, 12, 26, 37

Animals with two heads (and sometimes two tails and eight legs) are conjoined twins. They seldom live very long. There are more two-headed sheep than, say, two-headed elephants, because ewes often give birth to twins.

Vault p. 38

An underground strong room. In old buildings such as churches, the rooms below ground level would have vaulted ceilings—arches that meet at a central point—to bear the huge weight of stone above them.

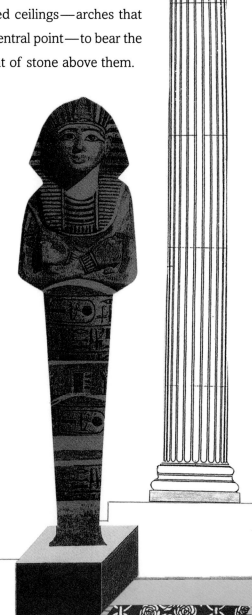

Index

rocke t

Jan Mark was one of Britain's most distinguished authors of books for young people. She was twice awarded the Carnegie Medal and also won the Penguin *Guardian* Award, the *Observer* Teenage Fiction Prize, and the Angel Award for Fiction. Jan Mark passed away in January 2006.

Richard Holland says that *The Museum Book* inspired him to work in a new illustrative style. "To reflect the historical aspect of Jan Mark's text, I adopted a mixed media approach using print and collage. It was an illustrator's dream." Richard Holland received a BA in illustration from Loughborough University and now lives in Essex, England.